1

2023 年
the year 2023

a small catalogue of thoughts
on wisdom and stupidity
while traveling

by sabina petra

4

Book Cover by Sabina Petra / Photographs by Sabina Petra

1st edition 2025

ISBN 979-8-9926389-1-2

1. 春 (spring)   ten poems

2. 夏 (summer)   ten poems

3. 秋 (autumn)   ten poems

4. 冬 (winter)   seven poems

1. 春 (spring)

manila
seoul
mumbai
and a memory of kyoto

one.

why don't people say what they mean?

it's because no one does
and when no one does
you fear that everyone you're honest with
disappears

so you're quiet
as you follow their quiet
and the world
stands still

two.

standing on a singular patch of dirt
doesn't make you a tree
you have to connect to so many things around you
in order to produce a leaf

three.

have you ever been overwhelmed?
your senses stop working for you
to start working against you all at once
everything becomes bright
loud
painful
the world turns from a brilliantly colored fabric
to a bucketful of needles

the sun beating on my shoulders
the heat sucking out the last drop of sanity
the trash the smell the glare
the people the stares the yelling
the honking the cars the mopeds the motorbikes
the streets get narrower
friendly voices seem to drown
in a sea of chaos
my brain is pounding
get out get out get out

and i want to cry
i want to cry because i understand i am missing out while i am
panicking
i want to cry because i have no control over my senses
and no control over the world
i want to cry because i want to be somewhere cool and quiet
i want to cover my ears and sit in a corner

i want to hold your hand on the top of the william wallace monument
it's just you and i and the green hills and the chilled wind
you squeeze my hand so hard it almost hurts
to remind me that you are here and you will not let go
no matter what
and if i doubt even that,

you will add your arm and the length of your body to that promise
you will add the warmth of your lips on my hair and the whisper of
your voice
you will be there for as long as it takes for the world to return to me
for me to return to you

i calmed myself down thinking of you that way
but on this horrible day
you were the most absent you've ever been

many people leave
but i will not
i don't want to be the person who is
absent

four.

무
my soul is like a radish
looks sweet tastes sharp
blood purple skin and pure white heart
you could cut it open like a flower
with sharp elegant edges
expose the fruit
but that takes skill
i can't seem to do it

five.

i'm in a constant state of being lost and found
lost and found
i know so well who i am
and what i want
and the nearness of one of these
might be the loss of the other

six.

i love them
the two brothers
about 7 and 11
identically dressed
identical birth marks
their eyes crescent moons with quiet laughter
whispering jokes and
holding hands like partners

the man who playfully rubs his wife's head
tells her to not look at the ground so much

the young girl who asks me where i'm from
5 years old and better at english then most
much better than when i was 5

the woman with the bright red cheeks and the
peach fuzz skin
the child with her bare feet on the wooden floor boards
soft as moist sweets

the boy swinging his bat over and over
i mimic throwing a ball at him
and he cracks a smile so wide
he looks like a different person
beautiful white round teeth
and rich soil eyes
     nice
i say
     nice
he repeats
the foreign word savored on his tongue

the woman who sells me tea
        you like green?
she says
eyeing my coat and my bag and my shoes
        yes
i laugh
        <u>midori</u> everything

i love the tall dads with their shiny, floppy hair
with their long legs and their ever-young sneakers
running after toddlers

i wonder how they live
how love feels to them
i wonder if they remember me as fondly

seven.

he can't be more than 21
tops
he's sprinting up the garden path in his cloth ninja shoes
and his high collared dark blue sweater
a large bag full of twigs and bark slung over his back
bounding up the steep hill like it's nothing
his black hair gleaming in the sun

on his way back he shyly greets me
charcoal eyes and rosy cheeks
it's cold
full lips
gosh you're cute

it's funny
being a gardener in a buddhist temple
building things to grow and last
cultivating heaven
when the faith acknowledges you own nothing
have no control
and everything is fleeting

eight.

a beautiful man
tall
a sweep of hair so black it's blue
chiseled face
full lips
deep brown eyes
an easy swagger
a sense of style
is making his way towards me
by his side is a woman
skin like porcelain
hair like silk
a waist cinched to the heavens
tattoos and edge and beauty
they are not touching
but they are obviously together

the man stares at me
openly
while the woman is looking at her phone
he stares
not with admiration
nor with judgement
but a sort of confusion
as if i have just appeared to him out of thin air
or as if he's never seen anyone like me before

i like to think i'm special
but in the end i'm just a regular blonde white woman
with a few extra pounds hitchhiking on her midriff
bright eyes maybe
bright light on the inside
but no model material

and he stares
he doesn't look away until we've crossed paths and
i can't see if he's still looking
if we had stood still we would have just been
eye-locked
looking at each other as if
he's asking me a question
and i'm about to answer

and maybe later
when the day is done
and the lights are off
he might allow himself to wonder
what my lips feel like against his

nine.

every love i've had
is like the first
it's the first of its kind
i remember all of them
the real ones
imagined ones
the fervently wished for ones

the one when i was 4 years old
i filled at least 3 diaries with hearts and prayers
is that technically the first?
the one where i was asked for the first time
to go steady
and was so surprised i said
      yes!
at 7
was that it?
the one where i was truly head over heels
my first lips-only kiss
at 13
the one where i first felt loved
first french kiss
18
first sex
19
which was so wonderful that i've never stopped wanting more
my first same gender adventure
which taught me a lot of things
including independence
guilt, shame
resolve
and identity

21

then my first - and only - marriage
which was hopeful
but not love - not really
it catapulted me around the world
my first friends-with-benefits
which absolutely crushed me
my first being treated like royalty

as wonderful of a thought it may be
to have one person thread through your life
it's not true
it's a strangely woven quilt
a long necklace of memories
every day a new bead

ten.

you are
so beautiful
i want to run my hand through your thick curls
big as hoops
so jet-black a sharpie must have colored it in
i see 1 gray hair dancing through it
but you can't have reached 30 yet
your skin is like caramel cream
your eyes like 2 small sage leaves
sharp as knives
filled with coffee beans
a high blush in your cheeks
and that's all i can see
those damn masks
i want to see your smile
if i could

you look at me
shocked, affronted, interested?
that strange woman in her bright clothing
calm in demeanor and loud in presence
when you are so collected and cool on the outside
yelling on the inside

we get off at the same spot
and make our way to our connecting trains
i'm not fast but way faster than you
and i lose you right away
what a beautiful second it was

my train is waiting for me as i get to the platform
i hastily hop in
and as the doors close

there you are
ambling onto the scene
you have a destination but no purpose
those curls springing up in joy
where your heart should have some
my train departs
into the opposite direction
of you

goodbye

2. 夏 **(summer)**

new zealand
seoul
macau
lynchburg, va
and a memory of kyoto

one.

oh the mountains
and the water
are making me cry
they keep being
so beautiful
over and over
and over

two.

it is not all that bad
to fail
you can chalk it up to a bad turn
try again later

but to fail at something you thought you were good at
at something you know you are good at
something you've boasted about
instilling as much faith in others as you have stored in yourself
to take on responsibility
and then let a whole slew of people down

that
that is phenomenally uncomfortable
embarrassing
painful
humiliating

i hate being bad at things
it is something i absolutely despise
i cannot tell you how many tantrums i've thrown
because the ability seemed to be slipping through my fingers

i cannot stomach
not doing something well
why isn't it flowing freely from my hands?
i know i have skills
so why am i not able to use them?

what if everything
i think of as attainable
is in fact so difficult
i will never do it perfectly?

i only know i have to try
i have to get up and keep trying
i have to keep going
because a life without attaining the perfect thing
knowing i can do it
is inconceivable

three.

if i can have an image of my life
to look back on when i get the rundown in heaven
can it be of my falling backwards on the made-up bed
my legs held high so that
my pant-legs would fall back with gravity
in order to rub in the cream i already had on my hands
i slide my hands over the smooth surface and all the way up to my feet
i feel agile like a baby
and happy i get to do this together with my body
go team!
as the autumn sun whispers through the leaves!

four.

i feel like a balloon
my body tethered to the world with a thin string
one snip and i'll be loose
my mind ruffles with every gust of wind
my eyebrows like small ballast-weights
drooping to the floor

i wonder if this is all anxiety
pure fear
and i can't even pinpoint what for
simply afraid
of what's to come
while i cannot stay here

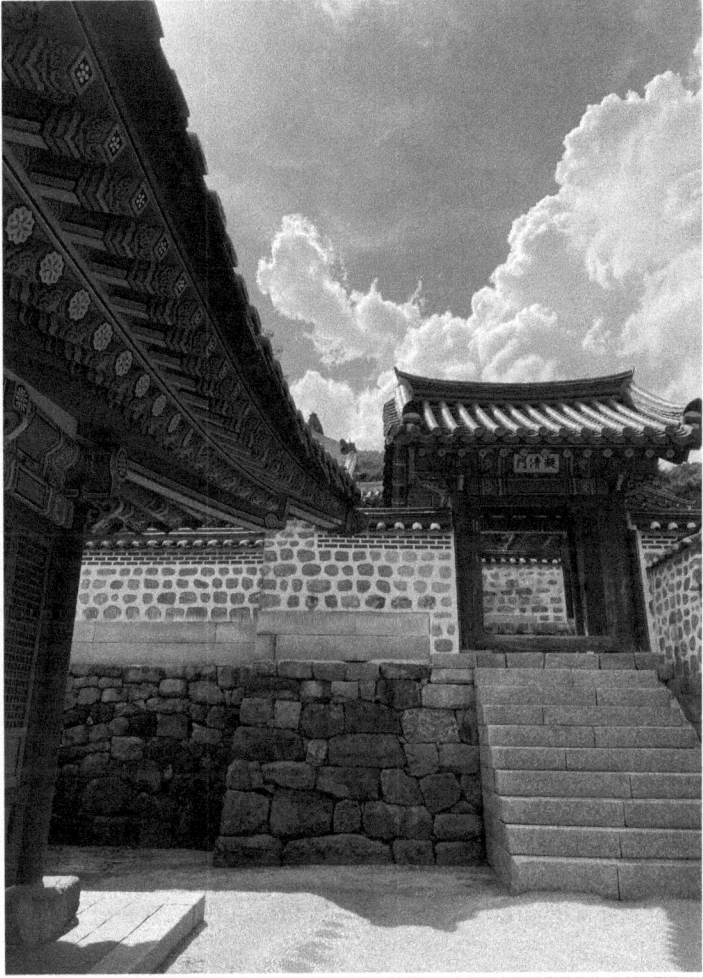

five.

this time might be confusing
encroaching
strife and uncertainty from every corner
emotions vying for attention
but
if you can
try to savor this feeling

you will feel certain
and clear headed
happy and strong
very soon
your current state will fade and a new one will arrive
it's inevitable
and you will not even understand how
you were able to feel this lost
but
this feeling
is a shade of who you are
simply a different color
and you get to experience this turning of your leaves
from green to gold to brown to gone
even in its sadness
it's beautiful
so savor it
it is a wondrous and humane state of being
a new season will come
and although you'll be grateful for snow and fresh flowers and poolside
days
you will crave a pumpkin spice something soon
we all do

six.

oh i remember this
the warm tarmac of the last days of summer
the dead leaves still hanging onto the trees for dear life
the crickets yelling at each other in a constant drumming
the grass wet from a rainstorm forgotten
the pitch dark of the night in the suburbs
a deer munching on the neighbor's azalea bushes

i remember this feeling
walking down the road back to the apartment
4 beers deep and a faint smile on my lips
i remember loving you like this -
through these surroundings alone i can almost
hear the faint clinking of glasses
see the snailing smoke of cigars -
and on cue
your face swims into focus in the pool of my mind

this is where i spent my months
in the south of the united states
loving you from afar
holding you so close in thought
skin-tight
wrapped around me like blood vessels wrap around muscles
while you were physically
planet-loose
expanding like the universe

i laugh now
thinking about us
we are so incredibly different
you are tightly wound like a coil of copper thread
humming with thoughts until a spark of electricity

forces it out of you
like a shout
and i am open like a packet of sweets
multi colored toffees spilling out for everyone to feast on
like laughter

and maybe that polar opposite life
is what will keep the connection between us taut enough
for a little bit of love to tiptoe across it
for as long as we live

seven.

my favorite are the zen gardens
because they somehow make me think
of nothing
not what i should solve
or be
or think
not what i should do
achieve
travel to
there is a blank slate
at that garden
simple lines and snow capped roofs
a warmth within
a breath

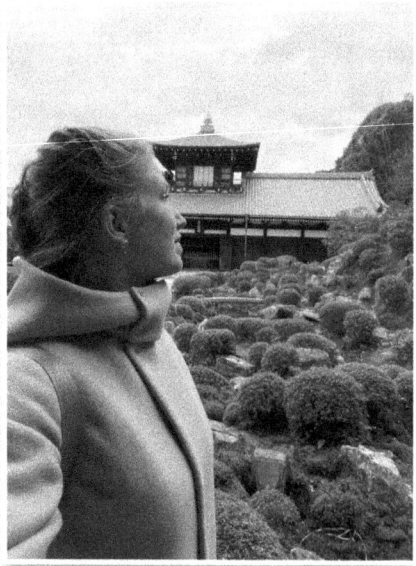

37

eight.

i look up and maybe for the first
time in my life
i notice a boy with eyes like mine
he walks upright
with purpose
and he's youthful
there's joy in his limbs
but his eyes
have anguish
there's strength in anguish
it's not simply sad
it's pain
and pain will birth something
his eyebrows are furrowed
a covid mask hiding the rest of his face
i wish he'd see me
and recognize my eyes for his

nine.

it's too bad you only see a part of me
the loud jolly part
the singing laughing yelling performing part

but here we are
you and i
midnight and
only a piece of plywood and wallpaper between us
we might be even sitting back to back
and we wouldn't even know

i'm thinking of you
you might be thinking of
your family
tomorrow's work
money worries
a creative endeavor
heartbreak
erotic fantasies
or
nothing at all
or
me
knowing i am right beside you
in this bed
clothed in the hotel's bedsheets
thinking of you

but what about me would you think of?
besides my face and my bright green coat
besides my loud laugh and my piercing voice
and the two dutch words i taught you
you don't know me

it's too bad that you don't get to see
the quiet
soft side
the loving dreaming worried childlike hopeful
the touching pondering wondering frowning scared
sheltering shelter giving brave kind temperamental part

i wonder if you'd like me more
i wonder if you'd think of me now
if you're not already
asleep

ten.

i have three weeks left,
to find my peace
to find an incredible joy in the smallest of things

because that's the way of japan

unexpected sunshine in the morning
gardens with bright green moss
a tucked-away café with funky music
where the barista smiles at me,
and lets me sit for an hour with one pot of tea to read my book
a couple i keep seeing all day in different places
a gentleman painstakingly drawing a picture of the river
a woman feeding the neighborhood cats
red socks
a savory steamed bun that turns out to be sweet
orange leaves among the green
toilets everywhere and they're clean and the seats are heated
a beautiful tea cup
a kitchen with two elderly women making the most flavorful curry
noodles i've ever had
the street-corner with mysterious obsidian rocks in the dirt
kids throwing snowballs at each other and squealing
someone practicing the trumpet on a floor above me
remembering i bring my own instrument everywhere
floating a bamboo boat up the river for luck,
made by a man who gives them away for free, fleeting and perfect

everything is fleeting and perfect

43

3. 秋 **(autumn)**

lynchburg, va
zhuhai
shanghai

one.

often
the world tips
like a ship
i feel myself stumble
as the physical surroundings ripple like a wave

for a mere second
i forget what ocean i am in
whether i am at the starting harbor,
the destination
or drifting out at sea
what time in my life it is or really
what life i am living
i forget and i
wonder if i am crazy or
if i am right

two.

Every morning I have a cup ready for tea. I love tea. Tea is my favorite thing.
This cup is enormous. It has big red flowers on it, a handle that can fit my entire hand, and the cup itself must be able to hold a gallon. Alright, maybe not a gallon, but close.

There is a tea bag in the cup. It is ready. It is waiting for hot water to be poured onto the teabag. In ancient Asian writings it is said:

> the act of the tea ceremony,
> is essentially to boil the water,
> make the tea, and drink it.

All I have to do to complete the ritual is to make the tea and drink it.

I never make the tea. I am in a land of teahouses and I never drink the tea.

I drink alcohol. Cheap fermented rice beer from the corner store, 1600 won, which comes to about $1.23 a bottle. I drink the beer and read my little blue book about Seoul and get lost in what could be.

Because tea - tea shows you where you are. Tea makes you aware of the moment you're in. The smell, the warmth, the calm.

Makgeolli, however, puts you in a place of where you want to be. It makes you yearn, it makes you think you've gained, think you should, think you can, think you will. It makes you dream.

And the thing about dreaming, is that you wake up in the now. Where you should have had tea.

48

three.

so far
no man
has wanted to have a conversation
they want to preach
they don't want to kiss
they want to put their tongues in your mouth
they don't want to have sex with you
they want to get to a destination by taking the same route
who cares if they use a different vehicle
a plane can cleave an ocean, right?
a ship can weather the clouds
they think they know their way around the world so well
of course they don't need to ask for directions
of course they will take the lead on this
this planet has always worked this way
the man starts out and the woman will follow
such fucking bullshit

but
like i've been taught
like i've been shown my whole life
i do
i follow
i mean
he ordered a taxi
he gave me something to eat
it is only fair
it is only nice

why do i feel i owe him in some way?
was i selling him something?
did he pay for it?
did we close a deal? sign a contract? spit and shook hands?

give him a chance
just because he's poor
or young
or doesn't really hold the same interests
or values
can't look you in the eye
seduces you by way of petting the space on the bed beside him
turns off the lights 10 minutes after you've met

and because he's cute
because i'm lonely
because i haven't been touched in
because i haven't touched anyone in
because i've put effort in
because i've put hope into
because i've come all this way
i might as well

i am a grown woman
i have a job
i have worked hard
i have a nice hotel room waiting for me
with a rain shower
i have a good brain nestled in my head
and yet

when i step into a situation where i know immediately
that this is below my level
that i deserve better
i stay

because it's nice to do so
because i am a nice person
let's not hurt anyone

unless of course
i'm hurting myself
in which case it's fine

51

four.

i thought of you
and my heart quickened

but i couldn't give my body
my whole body over to the thought
the image of your smile
or your lustful gaze
your hands your chest your breathy voice

i wondered why but in the back of my mind i knew
i knew that if i did
i would break
break right down the middle
down that ridge in the centre of my brain
split clean like a walnut
tear down the dark recesses of my gut
zip open the mysteries that reside within

i would black out
my mind would leave my body
and float around in space
forever caught in the shower cabin i find myself in

perhaps i was dehydrated
and didn't have enough sleep
perhaps my heart is empty
sucked dry in the last couple of days
perhaps the steam of the shower
transported me to dreaming

or perhaps
i came as close to you in your thoughts
as you came to me in mine
somehow

and the universe got confused
as to how we could be connected
인연
the brush of our skins
from worlds away

and there it was
my body was breaking
my mind split down the middle
like a walnut

five.

i don't know what makes me so afraid of sleep
i don't feel safe
as if i'm about to fall off a cliff
into a deep dark hole where
life happens to me
i know no one
can do nothing
there's no sense of direction
where i have no voice
no action
no consequence

no love

when someone else is beside me
i don't feel better
i teeter just as much

but what if you
particularly and specifically you
were beside me?
what if you slung your long arm around my waist and
placed your soft lips on the back of my neck
what if your breath made sure to match mine
what if your legs anchored me to a part of this world
what if your body was a buoy
and kept me afloat through all dangerous waters?
what if the pit didn't exist because when we fall off that cliff together
we either fly or swim?

what if you told me everything was going to be alright
and i believed you
because you aren't leaving?

six.

how wonderful
that i get to love you like this
like the man i imagine you to be

this man
does not exist
not within you

i know you
i know who you used to be
how you appeared solid
only to dissolve into smoke

i know you
i know who you are now
rooted to this soil
one track one thought one goal
the places you dreamed of will stay dreams
and happily so;
much better afloat in your mind than heavy in the palm of your hand
it is your choice
completely by force you see the world one way
the easy way

and who is to say
that easy isn't the best way to go?
easy is good
easy is smooth
you will always feel accomplished
no challenge means no chance of failure
nothing lost and nothing learned
life could be really good

but no
not for me
i want to learn many things
i want to grow and gain and see
which means i must also inevitably
diminish and lose and fall
because no one does something perfectly the first time around
you have to practice in order to see the
valuable and agonizing and astonishing things
i will live the hard way
or else i will keep asking myself
wether there is something i haven't felt yet
a part of me i haven't mapped out
a nerve i haven't touched

it is so wonderful to love you
as i imagine you to be
because i imagine a lot for you
even if you cannot

seven.

we all have so many scars
it is kind of funny and sad
how we keep them to ourselves
safeguard them
like little pilot lights
keep the flame alive so they can
warm our decisions in cold hearted circumstances

we could shed light on how similar we are
and how our troubles are not
as heavy as we make them out to be

but we like to be tortured
and special

and i personally
don't want to talk all day about what bothers me
or what bothers you
i'd rather find what gives us joy instead

but joy can be hard to find when
all your energy goes to guarding
that pilot light

eight.

it's just a character
you're just playing a character
it's not you
i know nothing about you

you're not this honest
funny
you're not this kind
or simple
you're not this hard working
this handy
you don't wear these clothes and
you don't hold these views
you don't have this past
this future
this life

the only thing i know about you
is the line of your jaw
the depth of your dimples
the gumminess of your smile and
the flop of your hair
the sound of your voice
the cadence of your words
the gait of your walk
the two moles on your cheek
the curve of your lips
the closeness of your eyes
that red dot in your left lower lid
the long muscle in your neck
the sharpness of your chin

the broadness of your shoulders
the long and slender upper body and the
shorter curved legs
the long fingers
the smirk
the whisper
the tease

they can all be used in a million different ways
ways i would hate
ways i would love

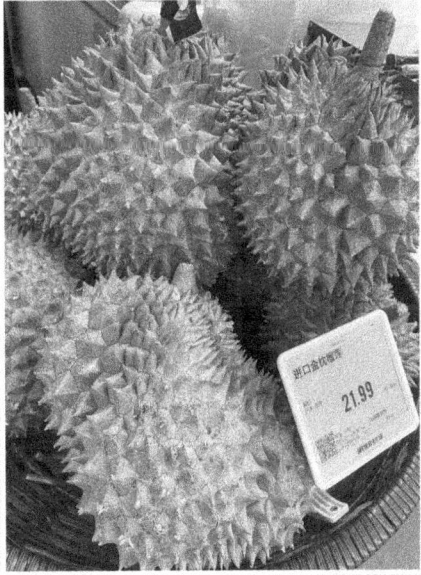

nine.

if you are never curious
as to what could challenge you
evolve you
what could inspire you or
leave you awestruck
does that mean
that nothing moves you?
and if nothing moves you
not even i
looking at you with all the love in my heart
bursting through my eyes
then
why are you alive?

living then becomes
a day to day thing
you're the king of your own small paradise
that never changes
no surprises
no disappointments
no strokes of brilliance
a bodily exchange without getting the mind involved
a green field white fence blue sky kind of life
where you never get to see the golden autumn of death
or the bitter white of refilling your resources
no wet painful splash
bursting forth out of your little tulip bulb

my life feels sharp
and dangerous
full of hard edges and harsh winds
warm hugs and soft bodies and good whisky and blistering fires
beautiful food and strange words and wondrous stories

it's the stuff of long tales
that as you hear it
you wish you were living

everything moves me because
everything moves

ten.

now that the characters in the story have kissed
i've lost interest in watching it
not because the goal has been reached
but because i feel slightly cheated
they don't need me to root for them anymore
they have found each other
they can move on
i'm still here

4. 冬 (winter)

kyoto
shanghai
tianjin
chengdu
shenzen

one.

there is a place in korea
where tall trees line a quiet path
everything is linear about this place
the strong vertical trunks of the linden trees
the long road stretching out to a spot beyond the horizon

at that horizon there is a field
where you can rest during
your last days as dust on this earth
beneath a tree   '
that will grow as tall and vertical towards the heavens
as its brothers and sisters

i want to rest there
there
is where i want to rest
which is the most comforting and
most terrifying thought in the world

comforting because
i know now where i want to go
where i want to end up
where i want to rest my bones
terrifying because
how does one even think of
the days beyond one's life?
how do you think of getting to where you finish
and
how
am i going to get there?
which turns will i take now
to end up resting where i belong?

two.

what a shock
i'd given up on you
and then out of nowhere
you put yourself into the conversation
suddenly you're there
and you have things to say
to teach me
to laugh at
with your eyes crinkled up like almond slivers
pine needles of joy
your shy smile splitting your face
the three little earrings in one ear tinkling at me
where did that sudden play come from?
that curiosity?
i slapped your arm and laughed
i startled you
you almost went out the elevator on my floor
you forgot your time and place

i wonder if
you want to relive that time over and over
like i do

three.

sometimes being silent is easier
if there are no words
there will be no questions
and i won't have to explain
what cannot quite be explained
or at least
not explained away

sometimes silence is the only answer i have
to how i got here
or what i am
or what i want

to what pain is like
or loss
what loneliness is like
what passion feels like

sometimes silence feels at least
like i gave the answer to myself
the only person who truly deserves one

i understand that words are a salve
and that if they don't heal a wound
they will at least help grow a fibre
and another
and another
until there is a crust
and then a scar
and then
a vague memory

but words can be painful
like iodine

and silence is peaceful
like water

water makes blood run quicker
a red river flowing from my finger

four.

next to me
waiting for the subway
is a boy who pretends to be suave
he does it all correctly;
he stands up straight
his hair is clean and shiny
his clothes modern but muted
yet he's failing miserably
i can feel his heart flutter from here

everyone
everyone is wondering how they are being perceived
everyone wants to be admired
and as i stand in a train full of people
i mean armpit to nose and
butt to laptop-case
i find that we're all extremely ordinary looking
who made us think the world is made up out of perfect specimen
and we are the only ones out of line?
the specimen are out of line and we
we are the truth
you have to dig deeper to get to beauty
but it's real
not made in a doctor's office or a make up studio or an editing room

we sway on our way to our daily duties
everyone hoping and no one doing something about it
everyone looking at the sky and not flying
maybe that's what makes us ordinary

five.

i really wish i could cry
i think it would help me
i think it would release something
i am drunk on soju
i should be able to let it go

but there are no tears
i am not sad enough
i am longing
and longing is different
longing has direction
while crying is a release
longing has a purpose
and will know no release
until you've reached it

i am longing for you
for who i think you are
for what i think you can show me
for how i think you might love me
for how incredibly happy i will be
in that somewhat hysterical
can't-help-but-laugh kind of way
to have found you

six.

i look at his lean body
his nutmeg skin and almond eyes
his obsidian hair
he is sizing up two ladies in front of me
refined, small
quiet, precise, graceful,
like intricate porcelain
who would want this tall, loud
colorful giant
with that booming laugh and her
pine forest eyes?

someone
someone would
someone who is tired of porcelain
and is looking for a forest

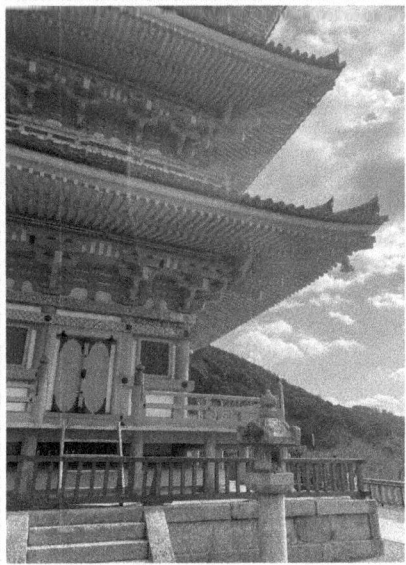

seven.

i remember standing in an airplane bathroom
crying
i had just said goodbye to my father i think
probably for good
i looked up at the mirror
into my own eyes
the green so bright it was almost turquoise
i remember thinking they looked like planets
in a young and freckled face
two big tears sliding down my cheeks

now
i cannot cry
my heart can tell
but my body doesn't show anymore
i have at once healed enough
and hurt too much
to allow myself to cry

as i look in the mirror
on this flight from DC to SF
i don't see the planets
i see the rings
the lines etched around my eyes
look where all that crying got me
it got me looking old
i am old
well
older
we never expect to grow old, really
we know we will
but we don't understand we do
theory and practicality are two ends of the spectrum

here i am
and the lines in my face cannot be erased by
a little make up
a cream
a good night's sleep
a glass of water
they will etch deeper with every flight i take

my lips are cracked and flaking
they haven't been kissed for too long
with intention

i'm proud of the years
and i mourn they've gone
so fast

please let me honor each day
thoroughly
if they're gonna be this precious

2023 年
the year 2023

a small catalogue of thoughts
on wisdom and stupidity
while traveling

by sabina petra

www.ingramcontent.com/pod-product-compliance
Lightning Source LLC
Chambersburg PA
CBHW072047040426
42447CB00012BB/3060